PREFACE

The last few years have seen a considerable growth in the provision of INSET, especially school-based INSET. Many teachers are now being asked to lead INSET sessions for groups of their colleagues, in both primary and secondary schools, and in all curriculum areas. The task of arranging, planning and leading a successful INSET experience for a group of colleagues is a new prospect for many teachers. This booklet is intended to give practical help and guidance to teachers who are beginners in the art of leading INSET sessions, either for colleagues in their own school or for broader groups of teachers.

The booklet is based on the work of the PrIME (Primary Initiatives in Mathematics Education) project, which worked from 1985 to 1989. As part of that project, about a hundred groups of primary teachers met at regular intervals to work on the teaching of mathematics. These group meetings gave the project team a unique opportunity to observe many INSET leaders of high quality at work. Their styles of leadership and their ways of conducting meetings were very different, but they won the cooperation, trust and commitment of group members. The ideas in this booklet are based on that experience of joining in the work of well-led groups of teachers.

The booklet was originally published as part of the PrIME project's INSET pack *Children, Mathematics and Learning* (published by Simon and Schuster, 1990). However, the booklet is not relevant only to INSET in mathematics for primary teachers; it may also be helpful to teachers who are leading INSET in other curriculum areas and with teachers of other age groups. Consequently, the booklet is also available separately; the two references within it to the PrIME INSET materials are only incidental, and the word 'mathematics' appears only once!

The project team hopes that the booklet will support teachers in the valuable and demanding task of providing opportunities for colleagues to reflect together on their teaching, and to develop their teaching skills further for the benefit of the children in their care.

Hilary Shuard
Angela Walsh
Jeffrey Goodwin
Valerie Worcester

WORKING WITH GROUPS OF TEACHERS

Hilary Shuard

Angela Walsh

Jeffrey Goodwin

Valerie Worcester

SIMON & SCHUSTER

LONDON • SYDNEY • SINGAPORE • TORONTO

The Primary Initiatives in Mathematics Education Project
was launched by the School Curriculum Development
Committee in September 1985 and completed under
the auspices of the National Curriculum Council in
August 1989.

National Curriculum Council
Albion Wharf
25 Skeldergate
York YO1 2XL

First published in 1991 in Great Britain by
Simon & Schuster Ltd
Wolsey House
Wolsey Road
Hemel Hempstead HP2 4SS

Printed in Great Britain by
St Edmundsbury Press
Bury St Edmunds

British Cataloguing in Publication Data

Working with groups of teachers
    1. England. Primary schools. Teachers. Professional
    education
    I. Shuard, Hilary   II. PrIME
    370.71220942

    ISBN 0-7501-0113-X

Edited by John Day
Designed by Danuta Trebus

Working with Groups of Teachers is also published in
Children, Mathematics and Learning, pages 11-21.

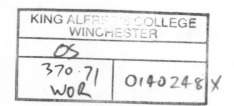

Introduction

This guide is designed to offer support and guidance to teachers who are new to the task of leading INSET activities. You may be planning to work with colleagues in your own school, or with a group of teachers from several schools, perhaps at a teachers' centre. The guide should help you to develop your ideas and your technique, so that you are able to plan and implement successful INSET.

Working with a group of teachers can be both a challenge and a satisfying experience. It can offer opportunities for the group to learn more about a topic in which they are all interested. It can provide an environment in which all members of the group, including the leader, can share experiences and ideas.

Working with a group of teachers may seem daunting to the new group leader. However, even a leader who is new to INSET has credibility by virtue of:

- Experience of working in the classroom.
- Experience of working alongside colleagues in school.
- Understanding of the INSET topic.

Reaching a full understanding of what is involved in leading INSET can take some time. As the group's way of working develops, so will your skills in working with the group also develop. The diagram shows some aspects of the role of an INSET leader. Which aspects do you feel it would be helpful for you to try to develop at this stage?

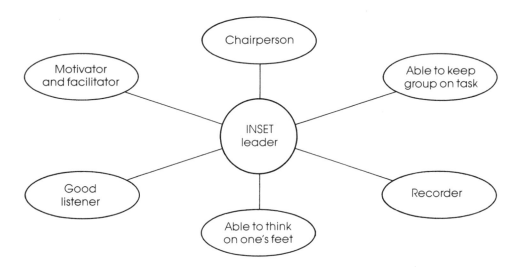

When you begin to lead INSET, it is important to feel as confident as possible. You should try to choose a topic and a range of activities which will fit in with your strengths. You should organise the session so that you feel comfortable that everything will run smoothly. If you can arrange to observe an INSET session led by an experienced leader, it may help you to focus on the role of the leader. If possible, sharing the planning and leadership of the group with a colleague is likely to help you, and to lessen your natural anxiety. Some suggestions for further reading about INSET are given at the end of this guide.

The next section focuses on some of the *practicalities* of organising INSET.

Preparing for INSET sessions

If the organisation of your INSET session is well planned, the group members are likely to develop confidence in you as a leader, and to join with enthusiasm in what you ask them to do. When the organisation is running smoothly, you will also have time and energy to lead the group sensitively and to respond to and build on members' ideas.

In planning your course, you should work through the suggestions below. However, not all the ideas may be applicable to your course; discard those suggestions which do not apply. There may also be other aspects of planning which you need to add to the list. For example, if you are going to use computers, you will need to organise this aspect of the work.

- Know the aim of each INSET activity that you are considering using.

- If you are using the PrIME INSET pack, decide which activities from the range offered you feel are suitable for the group's interests and needs. Also consider which activities are appropriate to your own skills as a leader, so that you will feel comfortable in carrying them out. For each activity, decide on a method of organising the group which is suited to that activity.

- Prepare for the whole INSET course by thinking through the aims of all the activities. Decide on some of the likely outcomes, and check that you have a coherent overall programme.

- Consider how the available time should be apportioned in each session. Make out a schedule of approximate times; this will help you to make decisions during the session. It will also aid in future planning, if other sessions are to follow.

- Make bookings of rooms, equipment and refreshments. If you are unfamiliar with the meeting room, visit it beforehand to check on furniture and equipment.

- Send out details of the meetings in good time. Include the venue, dates, times, and topics. List any materials and equipment which members should bring. Where necessary, give full directions for finding the meeting place; state where members should park their cars. It may be useful to give the starting time in this way:

    4.45 for 5.00; tea will be available at 4.45.

    This gives flexibility for people who are delayed. Give the finishing time as well as the starting time. If you are meeting as a school staff, it is still important for everyone to know where and when to meet, and what to bring.

- Check in good time that you have sufficient quantities of all needed apparatus and other resources. If not, you may be able to borrow what you need, or it may be possible for group members to bring their own resources.

- Ensure that you have all the documents and materials you are likely to need, such as sufficient copies of duplicated papers and OHP transparencies.

- Arrive at the meeting room well in advance, and check that everything that you need is available, and is in working order. Think about the ventilation. Check that there are enough chairs and tables. For a discussion meeting, arrange the furniture so that all group members can see each other. For practical activities, arrange appropriate numbers of chairs at each table. If an OHP or other display is to be used, make sure that everyone can see it.

- At the beginning of the course, make sure that group members know what is expected of them in terms of time and effort. At the start of each activity, make sure that group members know the purpose of the activity.

- If the group is newly formed, introduce yourself and have some name badges available. Alternatively, arrange an opening activity which gives group members an opportunity to introduce themselves.

You should now be in a position to feel that the organisation of the INSET session will run smoothly. You can now concentrate on other aspects of the role of the group leader.

Discussion and sharing of experience

Successful INSET often involves the sharing of experience, and enables group members to learn together while supporting one another. By the way in which you work with the group, you can create an atmosphere in which people willingly share their experience. The key to successful group work is the recognition that:

In group work, people need to work together.

From our everyday life, we know that there are skills which we use in different settings to keep channels of communication open. We also experience feelings of insecurity and nervousness in unfamiliar situations, and we learn how to cope with these feelings. You should now try to recall ways in which you keep communication open and overcome your anxiety in different settings:

- In the classroom.
- When talking with friends or colleagues.
- When meeting a class for the first time.
- In talking at a parents' evening.

These skills are the foundation of the group leader's work, and your experience in working with people has given you a good basis for using them. An important part of your role is to enable group members to share their experience and to learn from each other; for this to happen, the atmosphere needs to be supportive and unthreatening.

Successful group work is built on awareness of ourselves and of others in the group; we need to accept our own strengths and weaknesses, and to be sensitive to the strengths and weaknesses of others. This takes time to develop in a group, and first impressions often need to be revised. Different people bring different experiences and expectations to a group meeting. These expectations and experiences determine their interaction with other members of the group and their response to the group's activities. Working together enables us to learn more about ourselves, and to appreciate and understand other people better. This can help us to look at ways in which we interact in the classroom and with colleagues. The experience of group work may help us to have more patience, to listen more attentively and to respect the views of others. These ideas are discussed more fully in Unit E: *Managing Mathematics Learning and Teaching*, which uses PLR (Patience, Listen, Respect) as a framework for classroom work. It is equally applicable to working with groups of teachers.

For effective discussion to occur, the group size needs to be appropriate for the nature of the task. At different times the group may need to work in groupings ranging from pairs to the whole group, so that discussion can develop as a natural part of the activity. Both the chairing of a large group's discussions, and joining for a time in a small group's discussion, are part of the leader's role, and you will want to make these discussions as productive as possible. The following suggestions may help:

■ Ensure that the group size is appropriate to the task.

■ For small-group discussion, give a fixed time. You might say: 'We will come back after 20 minutes', or '... at half past two.'

■ During small-group discussion, spend some time with each group; try to help them to keep the discussion focused on the task.

■ State the reason for breaking into small groups. It may be to allow the sharing of experience among a small group, or to enable all group members to carry out a task. Some form of reporting back to the large group may be planned, so that all groups can share with each other. The method of reporting back will depend on the time available and the number of subgroups.

■ If small groups are to report back, each group may need a scribe to list a few points on an OHP transparency, or a reporter to give a general overview from the group. A few minutes before the end, remind the groups of the time, so that they can plan their report.

■ Remember that group members are unlikely to want to sit through reports of similar discussions by more than about three groups. Not all small-group work needs reporting.

■ When chairing a large group, act whenever possible as a listener and observer. Try to sustain the discussion and keep it focused on the issues. Plan how you will bring out significant issues for the group to focus on. If the discussion flags or departs from the topic, would it be useful for you to summmarise what has been said so far?

■ In a large group, how can you ensure that everyone who wishes to speak has a chance?

Dealing with problems and difficulties

In group work, situations may sometimes arise which make the leader's role difficult, or which raise questions about the group's way of working. These situations often make it necessary to think on one's feet, to re-organise the session, to adjust the timing, or perhaps to deal with situations in the group. You won't always get it right – no group leader always gets it right. Similar situations often arise in the classroom, and you have a great deal of experience of them. These situations vary from the tape-recorder not working to difficult problems with individual children.

The next subsection, *Problems and difficulties in INSET,* contains a list of problems raised by INSET leaders. Some of these leaders were very experienced, and others were new.

A way of trying to tackle some of these problems and difficulties is:

1   Sort the problems into two sets: those which relate to the group and those which relate to the group leader. Put each set into order, according to how easy or difficult you would find it to deal with each problem.

2   From each set, choose a problem which concerns you. Then concentrate on these problems; over several INSET sessions try to improve your skills in dealing with these difficulties. Feedback from a trusted friend in the group may be helpful.

3   Consider whether you have encountered any of these problems when you were a member of a group, or in leading a group. If so, try to recall how you felt about it at the time, and how the situation was handled. This may help you to work out possible courses of action. It may be helpful to discuss the situation with someone who has INSET experience.

Problems and difficulties in INSET

■   I find the group too big for useful discussion to take place. It might be useful to break the group up into smaller units, but I am not sure about the best basis for doing this.

■   I am not sure how to help to develop group interaction and a collaborative working style.

■   I can't seem to find a way of dealing with the person who talks and talks, and who takes over the group.

■   The group often seems to go off task. What can I do?

■   I wish some members of the group would think before they speak.

- Catering for the range of experience in the group is a real problem for me.

- I find it difficult to know how best to encourage the reluctant talker.

- They see me as the 'expert'. How can I encourage them to take responsibility and find their own solutions?

- If we all know each other already, won't that make real sharing threatening?

- One group of four seems restless and bored. Perhaps the tasks are not sufficently challenging, or are not related to their needs.

- As group leader, I feel that I can't let some statements go without comment, especially when I strongly disagree.

- I need to improve the organisation, and especially to get the timing right.

- As a new post-holder, I find running INSET rather threatening.

- I don't know how the group thinks the session is going.

- I know I talk and direct too much, but it is hard to change my ways.

An example of an INSET problem

As an example, consider the problem of the incessant talker. Jot down some ideas about how you might handle this situation if it occurred in your group. How does your list compare with the list below?

- Try to plan the task so that the amount of talking done by any one person is limited.

- Get each group member to write something down, and then ask for individual responses.

- Organise subgroups, so that the talker does not dominate the whole group.

- Sit next to the talker. He or she may not manage to catch your eye very easily!

- When another member makes a comment, say 'That's an interesting observation' and encourage him or her to take the lead.

- Keep the talker busy; make the talker the scribe or chair for the activity.

- Try, for some of the time, to seek comments from particular individuals, or direct questions to particular group members.

- Interrupt tactfully, suggesting that everyone should have opportunities to speak.

- Tactfully try to raise the problem of members who dominate the discussion; encourage the group to take control of the situation.

How did it go? Reflection and evaluation

The success of an INSET session depends on several factors, which include:

- Creating the right environment.

- Good group interaction.

- Worthwhile activities.

You will want to reflect, at the end of a session, on all these aspects.

You will also hope to feel positive about your own role as a group leader. It is necessary to recognise that the management and leadership skills of working with adults take time to develop; you should not feel too dispirited if it did not turn out exactly as you had hoped. An important method of developing the needed skills is to evaluate your work, and to reflect on what happened during the session.

There are two types of evaluation. 'Formative' evaluation takes place during a course, and involves you in reflecting on how the course is going. Formative evaluation helps you to respond to the group's needs in your planning for future sessions. If you are able to share the leadership of the group with someone else, you will both be able to make constructive comments, which will assist with future planning. If you are the only group leader, you can still use your reflections on what is happening to guide your planning.

'Summative' evaluation takes place at the end of a course; it helps you to develop your skills as a group leader for the future. In your previous experience as an INSET group member, you may sometimes have been asked to make comments about a course, and to say what you have gained from it. In other words, you have helped the group leader to evaluate the course. Asking group members to reflect on their experiences is a useful method of evaluating a course. Evaluation helps group leaders to find out about the effectiveness of their leadership, to consider how far the aims and objectives of the course have been achieved, and perhaps to discover how much individual group members have learnt.

If you ask yourself the following questions at the end of a session, the answers will help you to develop your skills as a group leader.

- How far have I achieved my aims?

- What have I learnt?

- How effective were my planning and preparation?

- What improvements should I make next time?

- What advice would I share with other INSET group leaders?

You can investigate the feelings of group members about the success of the in-service activity by asking them questions such as these:

- In what ways did the INSET material help us?

- Did the sessions meet the planned objectives?

- What were the most important issues raised?

- What were the most valuable parts of the course?

- What were the least valuable parts?

- Were any important aspects of the topic left out?

If you lack the confidence to ask the group these questions orally, a questionnaire (filled in anonymously) is a possible substitute.

Looking forward

You may be a new INSET leader, but you are an experienced teacher, and you know that many aspects of your teaching have developed since your first year of teaching. Your confidence, the effectiveness of your organisation and planning, and the quality of the relationships you build up with colleagues and children are all much greater than were those of the probationary teacher you once were. In the same way, your skills as an INSET group leader will develop and change over time, and you will probably gain more and more satisfaction from working with colleagues. Mutual trust between the participants in any group also takes time to develop, and many of the difficulties which group leaders encounter in INSET occur when group members are strangers to one another, or when the group is trying to 'find its feet'.

The composition of INSET groups varies greatly, as do the needs of group members. Some members will be volunteers, but others may have been 'sent' by their schools; in school-based INSET, all may be required to attend, irrespective of their interest in the topic. If the group members are strangers to you, it may be possible at the beginning of the session to sense some of the reasons that made them come. Even if the group members are your colleagues, and you all know one another well, you may be able to find out what they hope to get out of the sessions. The responses of group members to the activities provided will be affected by the topic under discussion, by the time of day, and by whether or not they are volunteers. You should try to be realistic about what is possible, given the circumstances of the group meeting.

Certainly, INSET does not change teachers; if change does occur, it is the result of teachers changing their own thinking and their approaches. The leader needs to recognise that each individual takes something different from a shared experience. All the group members will decide for themselves whether they can use their experience to adapt, modify or rethink their ideas. A supportive INSET environment can only provide a setting in which this professional development can begin.

As an INSET leader, good planning and preparation will stand you in good stead. For each session, you should make sure that you have thought out the introduction, you should try to ensure that the activities are suitable for the group, and you should plan the timing to allow for summarising or feeding back the main points. Be prepared to be flexible and to negotiate in response to the group's needs and wishes, so that the pace is acceptable to them. However, a deviation from your plan is not a failure on your part; opportunities for the group to engage in collaborative ventures and discussion are very important. Remember that sharing a problem or a success is worthwhile, and that INSET discussions give teachers opportunities for sharing which do not always occur elsewhere in the hurly-burly of school life.

Further Reading

Button, L. (1981). *Group Tutoring for the Form Teacher. 1: Lower Secondary School.* Hodder and Stoughton

Button, L. (1982). *Group Tutoring for the Form Teacher. 2: Upper Secondary School.* Hodder and Stoughton

Eason, P. (1985). *Making School-Based INSET Work.* Open University/Croom Helm

Evans, M. & Satow, A. (1983). *Working with Groups.* Tacade

Hall, E. & Wooster, A. (1984) *Human Relations in Educational Settings.* Study Guide no 6. University of Nottingham School of Education

Rogers, C. (1983). *Freedom to Learn for the 80's.* Charles Merrill